My Visit to Mono Lake

a children's book

by

Monica Jones

with

David Carle

Copyright © David Carle
All rights reserved

ISBN-13: 978-1467953245
ISBN-10: 1467953245
Printed in the United States of America
First Edition 2011

Phalarope Press
carle@qnet.com
PO Box 39
Lee Vining, California 93541

DEDICATION

To the dedicated, hardworking rangers, naturalists, and seasonal aids who have worked for over 30 years at the Mono Lake Tufa State Natural Reserve.

ALL SALES OF THIS BOOK SUPPORT THE MONO LAKE TUFA STATE NATURAL RESERVE
THROUGH THE FRIENDS OF THE MONO LAKE RESERVE

Mono Lake Tufa State Natural Reserve: http://parks.ca.gov/?page_id=514

Friends of the Mono Lake Reserve: www.visitmonolake.org

CONTENTS

1. STRANGE WATER — 8
2. WHAT IS A TUFA? — 12
3. STRANGE LIFE — 15
4. A GAS STATION FOR BIRDS — 20
5. VOLCANOES — 26
6. YOSEMITE, BODIE AND LUNDY CANYON — 28
7. RANGER TOURS AND VISITOR CENTERS — 31
   NEW VOCABULARY WORDS — 32

ACKNOWLEDGMENTS

Thanks to David Marquart and the State Parks staff who keep the State Natural Reserve going against all odds; the Mono Lake Committee for their everlasting support for Mono Lake and environmental education, and the Mono Basin National Forest Service Scenic Area and Eastern Sierra Interpretive Association staff. Also to Claire and Susan Desbaillets, Kathy Duvall, Sally Gaines, and Janet Carle for helping with the text and cover.

Winter on the west shore of Mono Lake

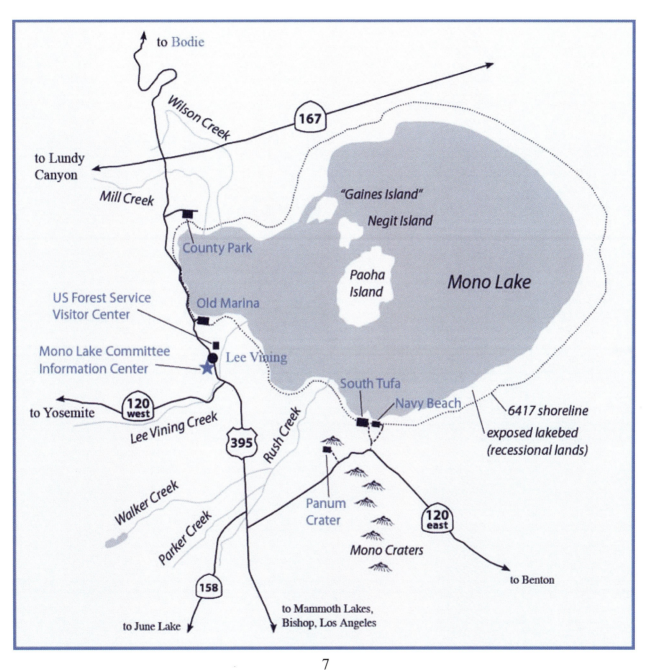

1. STRANGE WATER

Mono Lake is a gigantic salt lake east of the Sierra Nevada mountains of California. Park rangers there taught me all about the strange water, about rocks called tufa towers, and animals and birds that live in the lake during each season of the year. Mono (pronounced "mō-nō," not "maw-no") Lake is a special place, not like anywhere else. Even though my family lives hundreds of miles away in Southern California, where I am in the 4th grade, some of our water comes in long-distance *aqueducts** from streams that flow to Mono Lake. I learned how important it is to not waste water in the city to help protect the life of the lake.

    The first place I visited was the South Tufa Area and the first thing I noticed was how quiet it was there; the wind blew softly

*see "New Vocabulary Words on page 32

and the only other sound I heard was the squawk of seagulls. Seagulls, here? Hundreds of miles from the ocean?

Yes! They are called California Gulls, and they live at the ocean in the winter, but fly here every summer to raise baby chicks on islands in Mono Lake.

Mono Lake feeds LOTS of birds. To

understand why, a ranger first told me to feel the water. When we rubbed it between our fingers, it felt slippery, like soapy water. We tasted our wet fingers and they were super salty. Where waves

splashed along the shore, white soap suds formed.

Later, I floated in the water on my back and it held me up – all those salts in the water will not let you sink!

The ranger gave me a recipe for mixing up salty, soapy Mono Lake water from things we have in our house:

MONO LAKE RECIPE

1 quart of fresh water
2 1/2 Tablespoons of salt
5 Tablespoons of baking soda
2 teaspoons of Epsom salts
a pinch of borax
a pinch of detergent

Mono Lake and ocean water are salty for the same reason: salts wash in from the land and build up because no rivers run out of the lake or the ocean. *Volcanoes* erupting near Mono Lake in the past also added to its special mix. For more than a million years the lake gathered salts until it became almost 3 times as salty as the ocean.

It is the baking soda in the unusual recipe that helps make tufa towers in Mono Lake.

2. WHAT IS A TUFA?

Tufa rock forms when underground *spring* water comes up under Mono Lake and reacts with the lake water to produce *limestone*. As the springs keep flowing, towers grow upward beneath the lake. One winter I saw tufa forming just off shore, because a freshwater spring (red-colored because of bacteria) ran from the beach into the lake. Yellow bits of tufa appeared where the two kinds of water mixed. No tall tower could grow in such shallow water, but it was amazing to see how a rock can begin from water!

    I wanted a small piece for my rock collection but, with so many visitors, soon the towers would be gone, so the rangers protect them from collectors and from being broken by climbers.

New, yellow tufa forming where spring water runs into the lake.

Tall towers have to form in deep water, so why do so many now stick above the surface? Mono Lake used to be much deeper. Where cars park today at the South Tufa Area, they would have been under water 60 years earlier. The lake dropped and exposed tufa towers because Los Angeles diverted streams. Without flowing streams to replace *evaporation* by the sun, Mono Lake eventually lost half its water and, so, became twice as salty. The algae, brine shrimp, and flies were in danger of dying as the lake became TOO salty.

Fortunately, the Mono Lake Committee saved Mono Lake. They won court cases because state law says living lakes and rivers must not be killed when water is taken by cities. Meanwhile, rangers began their work at the Mono Lake Tufa State Natural Reserve and the Mono Basin National Forest Scenic Area.

A march in front of the Committee Information Center in the 1980s

3. STRANGE LIFE

Mono Lake's strange water is too harsh for any fish, but that does not mean Mono Lake is a Dead Sea. It is actually super-alive!

　　Food chains describe what-eats-what in an *ecosystem*, beginning with plants that grow using the energy of sunlight. In Mono Lake, *algae* plants are too tiny to see, but they turn the water green in the winter when nothing eats them. In the summer, the water clears up because algae is food for brine shrimp and *alkali* flies. California gulls love to eat both the shrimp and flies, and so do over a million other birds that fly to Mono Lake every year.

　　A brine shrimp is only about as long as my fingertip. "*Brine*" means "salty water," and these little shrimp are very good at living in Mono Lake's harsh saltiness.

Each summer, more than 4 trillion brine shrimp are in the lake: that is a number with 12 zeroes: 4,000,000,000,000. That's a lot of shrimp soup for birds.

From shore and later during a Mono Lake Committee canoe ride, I saw crowds of shrimp in places. Some were red, some were whitish, and a few were light green, depending on what algae they had been eating. All of them looked wiggly, with 22 legs for swimming and big black eyes..

    A ranger showed me how to tell the boys and girls apart: the males have "claspers" by their heads that look sort of like big mustaches, used for holding the female when they mate. This picture shows a male holding a female. She has a brown pouch (at the base of her tail by the male's head) full of tiny eggs.

    The ranger told me something else that is really cool: the *scientific name* for brine shrimp is <u>Artemia monica</u>. My name is Monica too, but this type of shrimp has that name

because it is only found here in Mono Lake: "monica" and "mono," get it? When I learned that, I began to care even more about Mono Lake.

At first I was not sure I liked alkali flies, because there are millions of them along the shore and they look a lot like pesky house flies. But the ranger showed me, by walking straight into a mass of them, that the flies do not like us! They just move away when you get close.

They crawl into the lake to feed on algae and lay eggs on rocks. A *larva* "worm" hatches from an egg and eventually it attaches a black *pupa* case to the underwater rocks where, inside, it turns into an adult fly that pops to the surface. Whenever a fly walks back under water, a bubble of air forms on oily little hairs around its body so it can breathe! Mono Lake just has so many amazing stories!

Besides food for birds, fly pupae were gathered by the local Kutzedika Indians, who dried and ate them. I tried just one and it tasted kind of buttery to me. Not bad.

This rock, with fly pupae attached, was underwater. The ranger carefully put it back after we finished looking.

4. A GAS STATION FOR BIRDS

Most of the California Gulls found in this state are born here at Mono Lake (there are lots of other types of gulls with different names.) Baby chicks are born in nests on the ground on islands in Mono Lake, where they are safe. When Mono Lake dropped so low, coyotes were able to reach the main island where the gulls nested and the birds panicked and left. That helped the Mono Lake Committee decide it was time to save Mono Lake.

Many other kinds of birds feed here, but my favorite are phalaropes. They are tiny shorebirds that fly here all the way from Alaska and Canada every summer, stay long enough to get fat, and then use that food-energy to fly to South America for the winter. Mono Lake is a gas station for *migrating* birds!

When they fly in a flock, phalaropes look like a big school of fish, turning together all at once. I wonder which bird decides when to turn and how the rest follow so closely?

This phalarope was spinning around in circles, looking kind of crazy. Can you see the water ripples around it? Spinning is a trick phalaropes use to catch more brine shrimp. See how it is staring into the ripples, looking for shrimp that were caught up by the swirling water?

The bird seen in greatest numbers at Mono Lake arrives at the end of the summer and stays into the fall. Eared Grebes *migrate* from Canada in huge flocks; sometimes Mono Lake has more than 1 million grebes here at once, spread out across the lake, looking like dark spots on the water.

Grebes dive underwater for their food, propelling themselves with lobed toes, instead of webbed feet like ducks and geese. Their red eyes help them see in the murky depths.

When winter comes, there are no more shrimp and flies in Mono Lake, so the grebes fly south to the Salton Sea and Gulf of California. Think what it might have meant to all those grebes and so many other birds that rely on Mono Lake, if people taking water had caused the lake to die. I'm really glad Mono Lake was saved.

Other birds you might see are shorebirds like these avocets looking for food under water.

Geese arrive in the fall and winter.

Osprey nest in the springtime on top of tufa towers. They are big hawks that eat fish, so osprey have to fly to nearby freshwater lakes for food.

One place at Mono Lake where I saw lots of birds was the State Reserve's boardwalk, which crosses a marsh below the Mono Lake County Park, on the northwest shore of the lake.

An osprey

Canada geese sometimes spend all winter at Mono Lake, but most migrate south where it is warmer and less snowy

5. VOLCANOES

A chain of young volcanoes south of Mono Lake is called the Mono Craters. Panum Crater, only 600 years old, is a mile from the South Tufa Area and the easiest to visit. It has lots of *pumice* and *obsidian* rocks. The obsidian is a black "glass" used for arrowheads by the local Kutzedika Indians. Pumice forms when hot melted rock is full of gas bubbles, so the cool, hardened rock still has holes and may be light enough to float in Mono Lake. A rock that floats! That is another amazing thing about this place.

    The big white island in Mono Lake is called Paoha and the black one is Negit. Both formed from volcanic *eruptions*. Black Point, on the north shore, erupted under Mono Lake when the water was higher, during an ice age. Narrow cracks on top are lined with limestone because the volcano was once under the salty lake. Eruptions gave Mono Lake water its unique blend of salts.

Paoha Island, the "white" island, is on the left, and Panum Crater is near the south shore, not far from the South Tufa Area.

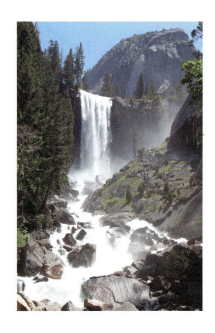

6. YOSEMITE, BODIE, AND LUNDY CANYON

There are lots of interesting places near Mono Lake. Yosemite National Park is most famous and has beautiful waterfalls, like Vernal Falls in this picture. One entrance to the park is only 12 miles from Lee Vining, the town near Mono Lake.

Bodie State Historic Park is north of Mono Lake, about an hour's drive (part of the way is a dirt road). Bodie was a big gold mining town in the 19th century and has been kept "in a state of arrested decay" since it became a park. That means they have kept it just like it was when people left (because the gold ran out) and Bodie became an abandoned "ghost town."

The mill at Bodie

Mill Creek runs into the northwest shore of Mono Lake, coming out of Lundy Canyon. There are campgrounds and a

reservoir there for fishermen, but my favorite things to do are hike up the canyon in the summer to look at wildflowers, and come back in the fall to see the aspen trees turn golden. Lundy Canyon also has waterfalls and even beaver ponds. I watched one evening as the beaver came out just before it got dark.

7. RANGER TOURS AND VISITOR CENTERS

I learned about Mono Lake on guided walks with rangers, offered daily in the summer. Good places to begin a visit to Mono Lake are the Scenic Area Visitor Center, at the north end of Lee Vining, and the Information Center (Mono Lake Committee) in the middle of town. I like to push the exhibit buttons at the Visitor Center and look for new books and T-shirts at the Information Center. Both have fantastic movies showing the area through each season and telling about saving Mono Lake.

    Someday I hope to be a ranger, because places like Mono Lake need people who care.

Photo credits: Mono Lake Committee, 14, 29; Mono Lake Tufa State Natural Reserve, 9 (gull chicks), 16, 17, 24 (avocets); all others David Carle; Map on page 7, courtesy of the Mono Lake Committee.

New Vocabulary Words *(italics in the text)*:

Aqueduct: a canal to move water a long distance

Algae: tiny green plants that can be seen in a microscope

Alkali: a base substance that dissolves in water and dilutes acids

Brine: salty water

Ecosystem: a community of plants, animals, and environment

Evaporation: the drying of water by sunlight and wind

Larva: fly eggs hatch as worm-like larva, which later form **pupae** cases where larvae become adult flies.

Limestone: calcium carbonate rock

Migrations: long-distance travels by animals to reach a nesting place or to avoid harsh winter conditions

Obsidian: volcanic glass used by Indians to make sharp tools

Pumice: lightweight volcanic rock

Scientific names: Latin names given to each plant and animal

Springs: where water comes up from below ground

Volcanoes: where hot, melted rock **eruptions** come out of the ground; rock cools, hardens, and builds mountains or islands.

Made in the USA
Lexington, KY
25 September 2014